From Kids with Love

Gifts Preschoolers Can Make and Give

Janis Hill and Laure Patrick

Fearon Teacher Aids
a division of
David S. Lake Publishers
Belmont, California

Dedication

To our families for their enthusiasm, encouragement and patience.

Acknowledgments

We are grateful to our family and friends who have assisted us with this book.

Thank you to:
Michelle Seeley, Bryan and Tracy Hill, Rikki and Emily Patrick, the Silvernail family, the Buelt family, the Deaton family, Penny Patrick, Macy Todd, Emily Anderson, the Masunaga family, Kristopher Zwetschke, Helen Pearson, David Pearson, Columbia River Council Girl Scout Troop No. 17, Creative Learning Cooperative Preschool, Trevor Perry, Madeline DeCourcey, Jason Vantine, Mashari Perry, and Tuan Tran.

Thank you to Kathy Mullane of Type Right for her professional assistance.

ISBN 0-8224-3166-1

Printed in the United States of America

1. 9 8 7 6 5 4 3 2 1

Contents

Introduction

- Children learn by doing.
- Children's self-esteem grows with each accomplishment.
- The process is as important as the product.
- Children need to learn the joy of giving as well as receiving.
- Child-created gifts are some of the most endearing presents loved ones will ever receive.

These statements are the basis for *From Kids with Love.* We feel it is important for children to actively participate in the gift-giving experience, so we have included over 70 ideas that give children between the ages of 3 and 7 the opportunity to create useful gifts. Some of these gift ideas will be new to you, while some are variations of old projects that emphasize child involvement.

Each project lists the materials and procedures necessary to make the gift. Many of the projects also suggest variations. The *Helpful Hints* sections that appear on most of the pages give ideas for working at different age levels. These ideas are based on our experiences with children. However, each child is unique, as are teachers and groups. As a general rule, never do anything for the child that the child can do alone. The finished products may not be perfect by your standards, but try to resist the temptation to "touch up" completed projects. After all, Grandma would rather have something her grandchild made than something made "perfect" by an adult.

Paper Gifts and Cards

Picture and Story Books

This is a story about my aunt Nancy.

I miss her and hope she comes to visit us soon.

At Christmas we can go to the beach.

suzi

This gift is one the child will love to see ten or fifteen years from now. It is especially nice to give to parents, grandparents, and teachers.

MATERIALS

For each book:

One 12″ × 18″ piece colored card stock or construction paper

Two 8½″ × 11″ pieces white drawing paper

Felt pens

Glue stick

PROCEDURE

1.   Have each child draw a picture of the person they want to give the gift to on one of the pieces of drawing paper.

2.   Have the child tell you a story about the person. Write it down on the other piece of drawing paper.

3.   Help the child glue the picture and the story to the card stock or construction paper. Fold the paper in half like a book.

4.   Write the child's name on the book and date it.

HELPFUL HINTS

For toddlers and preschoolers: To do this project the children need to be old enough to draw a little and verbal enough to talk about someone. A two-and-a-half-year-old is probably old enough to dictate a few thoughts about a close relative. You may need to ask specific questions, such as the following:

What do you like to do with this person?

What does this person like to do alone?

What do you like to eat with this person?

What do you do when you are at this person's house?

For primary grades: When the children are old enough to write, have them write down the stories themselves.

Picture Place Mats

Children love giving place mats, since they can be used meal after meal as a reminder of their giving.

MATERIALS

For each place mat:

One 12″ × 18″ piece construction paper

One 11″ × 14″ piece white or light-colored drawing paper

Two 12″ × 18″ pieces clear Con-Tact paper

Felt pens

Glue stick

PROCEDURE

1. Have each child draw a big bright picture on the drawing paper and sign his or her name and age.

2. Help the child glue the drawing paper to the construction paper. Allow to dry.

3. Cover both sides of the place mat with the Con-Tact paper. This works best when you have two people—one to hold the Con-Tact paper out straight, and the other to press it down slowly from one end to the other. If you have access to a lamination machine, you can use that instead.

VARIATION

• Make photo place mats by substituting pictures of family, child, house, or pets for the original art work. These work very well with toddlers, since they can help select pictures and spread glue.

HELPFUL HINTS

For toddlers: Young children will need encouragement to use a variety of colors. You will also need to help them write their names and ages.

For primary grades: These children might enjoy using their writing skills to complete the gift. The children can also help you cover the place mat with Con-Tact paper.

Woven Paper Place Mats

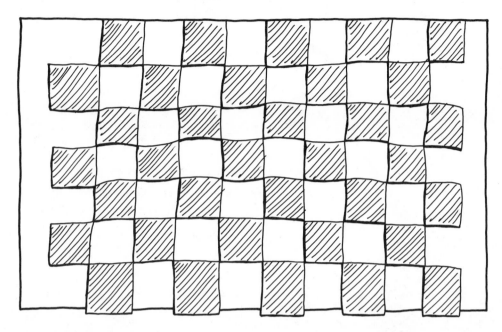

Children might enjoy making a set of these place mats for a festive family dinner or a holiday party. Try color combinations such as orange and black for Halloween or red and green for Christmas.

MATERIALS

For each place mat:

Two 12″ × 18″ pieces construction paper (Contrasting colors work best.)

Two 12″ × 18″ pieces clear Con-Tact paper

Glue or glue stick

Scissors

PROCEDURE

1. Fold one sheet of paper in half to 9″ × 12″. Draw a line parallel to the short end of the paper 1½″ from the edge.

2. Make parallel cuts from the folded end of the paper to the line you drew in step 1. (See Figure A.) The cuts should be about 2″ apart and there should be an odd number of cuts.

3. Cut the other sheet of paper in 1½″ × 12″ strips.

4. Have the child weave the strips into the large sheet.

5. Help the child glue the end of each strip in place.

6. Cover both sides of the place mat with the Con-Tact paper.

HELPFUL HINTS

For toddlers and preschoolers: This activity is not recommended for children under three. For preschool children, you should cut wider strips and make fewer slits to weave through. You also might want to mark an "X" on the places where the child should go over the paper. (See Figure B.) A child with some weaving experience should need the Xs only at the starting points.

For primary grades: You might want to have primary students weave with irregular shaped weaving paper or slits.

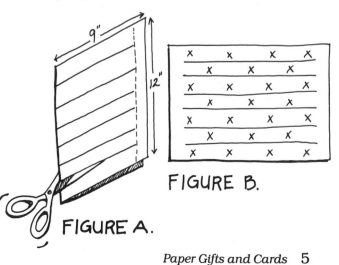

FIGURE A.

FIGURE B.

Scroll Wall Hangings

This lovely gift is easy to adapt for any grade level.

MATERIALS

For each wall hanging:

One 8″ × 18″ piece white or light-colored paper (A heavyweight bond works well.)

One 10″ dowel (¼″ – ½″ diameter)

One 12″ piece yarn or twine

Tempera paints

Flat-bottom containers, such as pie pans or cookie sheets

Glue

An assortment of stamping materials, such as cookie cutters, thread spools, and erasers

Newspaper

Paintbrushes (optional)

PROCEDURE

1.   Cover the work area with newspaper.

2.   Pour small amounts of paint into the containers. If the paints are too thick, thin with water.

3.   Have each child press a stamp in the paint and then onto the paper to make a design. Allow to dry when the design is finished.

4.   Help the child glue the paper to the dowel. The easiest way to do this is to cover the dowel with glue and roll the top edge of the paper around it. Hold the paper until set.

5.   Tie the yarn or twine to the outer edges of the dowel. The project is now ready to hang.

HELPFUL HINTS

For toddlers: If the children have trouble dipping the stamps in the paint, apply the paint with a brush and let the children stamp the paper.

For primary grades: Have children complete the activity by writing short poems or paragraphs about the designs or the recipients.

Picture Calendars

This original artwork calendar makes a lasting gift.

MATERIALS

For each calendar:

One 12″ × 18″ piece colored construction paper or posterboard

One 8½″ × 11″ piece white drawing paper

Twelve calendar grids with months and dates written in (See pattern on page 88.)

Felt pens

Glue or glue stick

Stapler

PROCEDURE

1. Have each child draw a special picture on the drawing paper.

2. Help each child fold the construction paper in half and then open it up. (Note: if you are using posterboard, draw a light line through the middle, rather than folding the board.)

3. Help each child stack the calendar grids on the bottom half of the construction paper or posterboard. Staple the pages to the paper.

4. Help each child glue the drawing to the top of the construction paper or posterboard. Allow it to dry.

5. Refold the paper with the picture and calendar inside, and have the child decorate the outside. (Note: this is not necessary when using posterboard.)

VARIATIONS

• Substitute photos of the children for the drawings.

• Use twelve pictures or photos, and twelve pieces of construction paper. Mount each picture on a separate sheet of construction paper with a calendar grid glued below. Stack all the months together with January on top and attach at the top with yarn or staples.

HELPFUL HINTS

For toddlers: This project may last several days. With supervision, young children can use one felt pen at a time to create an interesting picture. They can also help with gluing, stapling, and decorating the outside.

For preschoolers: With the exception of writing the months and the dates, preschoolers can master this activity with minimal assistance.

For primary grades: Have children write in the months and days. Older children can draw the grids using math skills.

Decorated Picture Frames

This decorative frame adds a nice personal touch to a child's photo or artwork.

MATERIALS

For each picture frame:

One white matboard frame (A precut matboard works well.)

A photo or a piece of artwork

Felt pens

Tape or glue

PROCEDURE

1. Have the child decorate the matboard frame with bright-colored felt pens.

2. Help the child place the photo or artwork in the frame.

3. Help the child tape or glue the outer edges of the frame together. This will keep the picture from slipping out of the frame.

HELPFUL HINTS

For toddlers: Scribbles will look beautiful with a young child's photo inside. Avoid the use of dark colors by not having them available.

For preschoolers and primary grades: Have children practice making designs on scratch paper first. Then they can transfer the best design to the frame.

Picture-Match Games

Children use original artwork to create a matching game for another child.

MATERIALS

For each game:

Twenty 3″ × 5″ pieces tagboard or unlined index cards

One Ziplock bag

Felt pens or crayons

Paper

PROCEDURE

1.   Have each child lay two cards down next to each other and make identical drawings on each card.

2.   Repeat this procedure for the remaining cards.

3.   Have the child make up some rules or instructions for you to write down.

4.   Place the cards and the game instructions in a Ziplock bag for storage.

VARIATION

•   Have children draw on only ten cards. Then photocopy their pictures, and glue them to the remaining ten cards.

HELPFUL HINTS

For toddlers: The photocopy variation would be best for this age group, unless the children can duplicate their work on another card. Encourage children to make a variety of designs by suggesting dots, squiggly lines, circles, and so on.

For preschoolers and primary grades: This activity can be adapted to the children's skills. For a simple game, suggest a single shape per card, such as a red circle, a blue square, or a green triangle. Children who are learning to count could make a game with a number on one card and an equal number of figures on the other. An older child might enjoy making cards with only a slight variation in each design.

Wallpaper-Match Games

Young children love to cut. This is a project that allows them to cut freely and use the pieces to design a game.

MATERIALS

For each game:

Twenty 3″ × 5″ pieces tagboard or unlined index cards

One Ziplock bag

Wallpaper samples (at least 10 different types)

Glue or glue stick

Scissors

Paper

PROCEDURE

1. Have each child cut small pieces of wallpaper samples. The shapes of the pieces do not have to be identical.

2. Place two of the cards on the desk. Help the child glue pieces of wallpaper to the cards. (The pieces should be cut from the same sample.)

3. Repeat the process for the remaining cards. Allow to dry.

4. Have the child make up some rules or instructions for you to write down.

5. Place the cards and the game instructions in a Ziplock bag for storage.

VARIATION

- Have children cut out similar objects from magazines. Substitute the magazine pictures for the wallpaper samples. The matching cards won't be identical, but the child receiving the gift can match a car to another car, a flower to another flower, and so on.

HELPFUL HINTS

For toddlers: You will need to discuss the concept of like and unlike things. Encouragement and reinforcement are keys to making this a successful activity and gift.

For primary grades: If you are using magazines, you might have children find pictures in challenging categories such as facial expressions which depict a wide variety of emotions.

Thumbprint Note Cards

These cards are a delight to make and to receive. You can add to the experience by pointing out that all fingerprints are different.

MATERIALS

For each set of four cards:

Four pieces heavy typing paper or quality drawing paper

Four plain envelopes

Stamp pad or watercolor set (See page 85 for homemade stamp pad recipe.)

Fine-point felt pens

One 18″ piece ribbon (optional)

PROCEDURE

1. Help the child fold the paper. Cut to fit the envelope.

2. Have the child make fingerprints or thumbprints on the front of the card. (If you are using watercolors, work some water into the paints before starting.) Allow prints to dry.

3. Have children decorate the prints with felt pens. They can add hats, arms, legs, feelers, wings, or anything that their imagination suggests.

4. Have children stack the cards and the envelopes together. If you are using ribbon, help them tie the ribbon around the stack.

HELPFUL HINTS

For toddlers and preschoolers: With young children we prefer to use the watercolors. It makes it much easier to wash!

Original Artwork Note Cards

Children can make these special note cards using construction paper, bulk stationery, or blank note cards.

MATERIALS

For each set of four cards:

Four pieces construction paper or bulk stationery, or four blank note cards

Four envelopes to match the stationery

Four pieces drawing paper

Felt pens

Glue or glue stick

Scissors

One 18″ piece ribbon (optional)

PROCEDURE

1. If you are using:
construction paper—help the child fold the paper. Cut to fit the envelope.
bulk stationery—help the child fold each piece of paper in half.
blank note cards—there is no preparation needed.

2. Cut the drawing paper so it is smaller than the folded card.

3. Have each child draw a special picture on the drawing paper.

4. Help the child glue the drawing to the outside of the card. Try to keep a margin around all sides of the drawing paper. Allow to dry.

5. Have the child stack the cards and envelopes. Either tie the cards together or wrap.

HELPFUL HINTS

For toddlers: Use a large piece of drawing paper rather than the precut smaller pieces. After the children have finished drawing, the pictures can be cut to fit several note cards.

For preschoolers: Some preschool children will need help cutting the drawing paper.

Melted Crayon Note Cards

These melted crayon designs add an unusual texture to note cards. Fancy seasonal cards can be made by mixing holiday colors.

MATERIALS

For each set of four cards:

Four pieces of card stock

Four standard-size envelopes

Four pieces drawing paper

Old crayons

Glue

Scissors

Foil

Paper towels

Sponge

For class use:

Warming tray or electric skillet

PROCEDURE

1.   Line the warming tray or electric skillet with foil. This will protect the surface from melted crayons.

2.   Turn the heat on to the lowest setting that will melt crayons.

3.   Have the child draw on the foil with crayons. Make sure that he or she does not touch the hot sides of the pan.

4.   Help the child lay the drawing paper on top of the crayon design. The child should use a thick sponge to press down the paper.

5.   Help the child pick up the paper and lay it on a flat surface to cool.

6.   Wipe off the foil surface with a paper towel and repeat the process.

7.   Fold the card stock in half, and cut to fit the envelopes.

8.   Help the child glue the crayon design to the front of the note card. Allow to dry.

9.   Have the child stack the cards and envelopes together and wrap.

VARIATION

•   Have children draw a picture on the paper first, and then place it face down on the foil. This will blend the colors slightly.

HELPFUL HINTS

For toddlers: This activity is not suitable for this age group.

For preschoolers and primary grades: Prior to beginning this project, review safety procedures. Both age groups will need adult supervision.

Cutout Note Cards

With the personal touch of a child's drawing and cutting, these simple cards become a priceless gift.

MATERIALS

For each set of four cards:

Four 8½″ × 11″ pieces colored construction paper

Four 8½″ × 11″ pieces white paper

Felt pens or crayons

Scissors

Glue or glue stick

PROCEDURE

1. Help the child fold the construction paper in half.

2. Help the child fold the front of the card in half again. (See Figure A.)

3. Have the child cut out a shape along the fold of the front of the card.

4. Open the card.

5. Have the child glue the white paper to the back of the construction paper. Allow to dry.

6. Refold the card in half. Have the child decorate the white paper with felt pens or crayons.

HELPFUL HINTS

For toddlers: Have children draw on the white paper before it is glued to the construction paper.

FIGURE A.

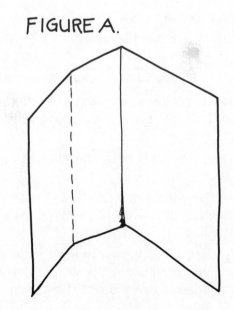

Cloth Gifts

Painted Fabric Banners

These bright banners are a good gift for a child to give to another child.

MATERIALS

For each banner:

One 12″ × 14″ piece solid-colored fabric

One 12″ piece yarn

One 12″ dowel (¼″–½″ diameter)

Several pieces newsprint

Chalk

Tempera paints or fabric paints

Paintbrush

Pinking shears

Glue

Tape

Newspaper

PROCEDURE

1. Cover the work area with newspaper and tape down.

2. Cut the edges of the fabric with pinking shears to prevent fraying.

3. Have the child draw several pictures on the newsprint. He or she should pick one picture to use on the fabric.

4. Using the draft as an example, the child should draw the picture on the fabric with chalk.

5. Have the child paint the fabric. Allow it to dry.

6. Help the child glue the banner to the dowel. The easiest way to do this is to cover the dowel with glue and roll the top edge of the fabric around it. Hold the fabric until it is set.

7. Tie the yarn to the outer edges of the dowel. The banner is now ready to hang.

HELPFUL HINTS

For toddlers: You might want toddlers to try making handprints or footprints rather than painting a picture.

For primary grades: You might have these children try two smaller banners that they can give as a set.

Felt Collage Banners

These beautiful cut-and-paste banners provide experience with texture and dimension.

MATERIALS

For each banner:

One 8½″ × 11″ piece felt for background

Several 8½″ × 5½″ pieces felt in assorted colors

One 12″ piece yarn or twine

One 10″ dowel (¼″ – ½″ diameter)

Scissors

Glue

PROCEDURE

1. Have each child cut out designs from the 8½″ × 5½″ pieces of felt.

2. Have the child organize the cutouts on the background piece of felt. The child should glue the cutouts in place.

3. Help the child glue the banner to the dowel. The easiest way to do this is to cover the dowel with glue and roll the top edge of the background felt around it. Hold the felt until it is set.

4. Tie the yarn or twine to the outer edges of the dowel. The gift is now ready to hang.

VARIATION

• Provide an assortment of different-textured materials to add to the banner.

HELPFUL HINTS

For toddlers: These children might have some problems cutting the felt. You might want to give them precut pieces to work with.

Fabric Bookmarks

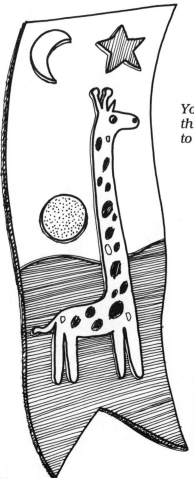

You might encourage children to think of tall, long, or thin objects to put on these useful gifts.

MATERIALS

For each bookmark:

One 3″ × 8″ piece burlap or felt

Scissors

Glue

Felt scraps in assorted colors

PROCEDURE

1.   Have the child cut out designs from the scraps of felt and fabric.

2.   Have the child glue the pieces to the 3″ × 8″ piece of burlap or felt.

3.   Help the child cut the bottom of the bookmark to make pointed, curved, or fringed ends.

VARIATION

•   Have children use fabric paints instead of fabric scraps to create their designs.

HELPFUL HINTS

For toddlers: These children might have trouble cutting felt. You may want to precut felt pieces for them to use.

Handprint Pot Holders

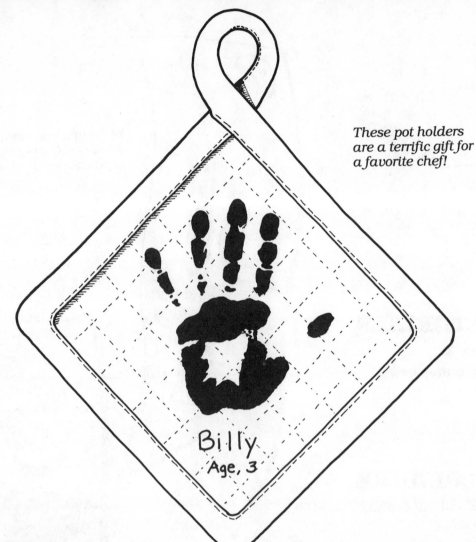

These pot holders are a terrific gift for a favorite chef!

Billy
Age, 3

MATERIALS

For each pot holder:

One homemade or purchased pot holder, solid light fabric

Fabric paints

Paintbrushes

Newspaper

Tape

Permanent markers (optional)

PROCEDURE

1. Cover the work area with newspaper and tape in place.

2. Tape the pot holder down on the paper.

3. Brush paint onto the palm and fingers of the child's hand.

4. Have the child carefully place his or her hand on the pot holder. The child should lift the hand off slowly so that the handprint remains on the fabric. Allow to dry.

5. Use a small brush to write the child's name by the print.

VARIATIONS

• Try a footprint for variety!

• Older children can decorate the handprints with permanent markers. Allow them to be creative.

Burlap Place Mats

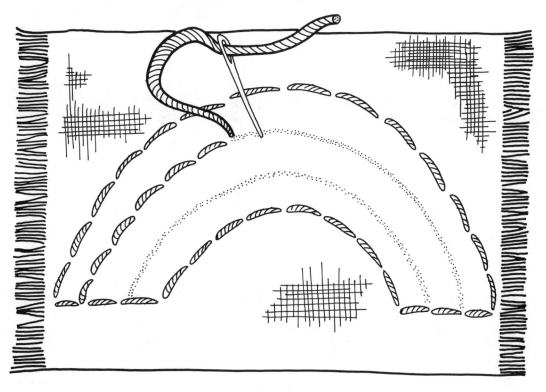

Burlap is a great material for beginning stitchers— the loose weave makes the sewing easy and the end product a success!

MATERIALS

For each place mat:

One 12″ × 18″ piece burlap

Large-eye blunt needle

Yarn

Masking tape

Permanent markers or fabric paints

Spray starch

Chalk

PROCEDURE

1.   Prepare the burlap by spraying it with starch and ironing it before giving it to the child. Fold masking tape around the edges to prevent the fabric from unraveling.

2.   Have the child draw a simple picture or design on the fabric with chalk.

3.   Have the child outline his or her design with a running stitch.

4.   The child can fill in the spaces with permanent markers or fabric paint.

HELPFUL HINTS

For toddlers: This project is not recommended for this age group.

For preschoolers: This project is best done over a period of days. Make sure the children's shapes are simple—a rainbow or a house are both excellent.

For primary grades: These children can use other stitches, such as the chain stitch, to fill in the open spaces.

Felt Coin Purses

Children find these difficult to give away. They might be the perfect gift for them to give to themselves!

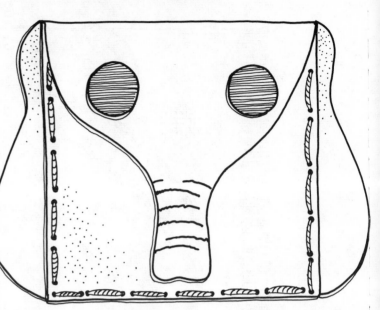

MATERIALS

For each coin purse:

One 6″ × 9″ piece felt

Large-eyed blunt needle

Coin-purse pattern (See page 89 for patterns.)

Snap

Embroidery thread (3–6 strands) or yarn

Pins

Scissors

Glue

Felt scraps

Hole punch

Buttons or plastic eyes (optional)

PROCEDURE

1. Have the child choose the pattern that he or she wants to use.

2. Pin the pattern on top of the felt, and cut out the shape.

3. Help the child punch holes in the felt where indicated.

4. Remove the pattern.

5. Help the child fold the piece of felt in half so the holes match. Thread the needle and have the child use a running stitch to sew the purse together. Help the child tie the knot.

6. Help the child fold down the flap piece. Attach a snap to the flap and the body of the purse to hold the purse closed.

7. Let the child decorate the purse with scraps of felt and buttons or eyes.

8. Have the child add a coin to the purse before wrapping it.

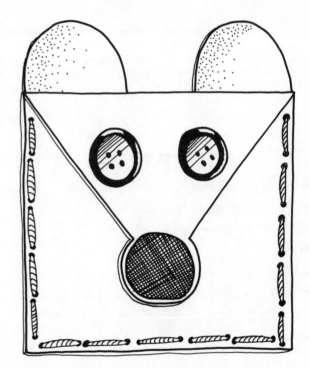

HELPFUL HINTS

For primary grades: These children can design their own purse patterns. You may have to help them cut the felt.

Embroidery Hoop Art

A child's bright picture, dressed up in an embroidery hoop and edged with lace, will accent any baby's or young child's room.

MATERIALS

For each picture:

One embroidery hoop (6″ diameter)

One 21″ piece eyelet lace (½″ wide)

One 8″ × 8″ piece white cotton fabric

Tempera paints

Glue

Paintbrush

Tape

Newspaper

PROCEDURE

1. Cover the work area with newspaper and tape it down.

2. Tape the fabric to the newspaper.

3. Have the child paint a design or picture on the fabric. Allow to dry.

4. Help the child place the fabric in the embroidery hoop.

5. Help the child glue the lace around the outer edge of the hoop as shown.

6. Trim the excess fabric.

VARIATION

- Have children draw a simple design on the fabric and outline it with a running stitch. They could fill in the spaces with permanent pens or fabric paint. You might want to lay the hoop down on the fabric and trace around it with chalk to provide a boundary for the children's picture.

HELPFUL HINTS

For toddlers: If toddlers have trouble painting on the small area, you could use a larger piece of fabric, have the children paint their pictures, and then cut it to fit in the hoop.

For primary grades: These children might want to make a draft before drawing their pictures on the fabric.

Puffed Pictures

*This stuffed picture is easy to make and gives
children a satisfying feeling of accomplishment.*

MATERIALS

For each picture:

One 10″ × 12″ piece solid-color fabric

One 7″ × 9″ piece white fabric

One 12″ piece yarn

Permanent markers or fabric paint

Cotton balls or pillow stuffing

Glue

Scissors

Hole punch

Newspaper

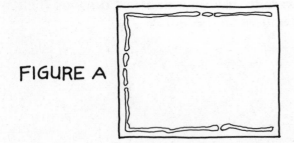

FIGURE A

PROCEDURE

1. Cover the work area with newspaper.

2. Have the child draw or paint a picture on
the 7″ × 9″ piece of fabric. Let dry.

3. Have the child put a thin line of glue on
three edges of the picture and glue it to the
larger piece of fabric to form a pocket as
shown (Figure A). Let glue dry.

4. Have the child put cotton balls or stuffing
inside the "pocket." Make sure he or she is
careful not to stuff it so full that the glue
comes undone.

5. Have the child put glue on the underside
of the open edge and press it down firmly. Let
the glue dry.

6. Punch two holes in the top of the larger
piece of fabric, and help the child thread the
yarn through the holes. Tie in a knot at the
top.

Gifts from Nature

Leaf-Print Note Cards

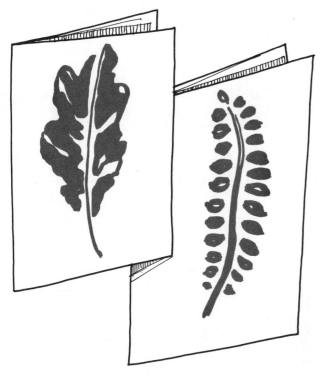

These detailed, delicate prints are easy to make. If you can, take children on a nature walk and let them collect their own leaves.

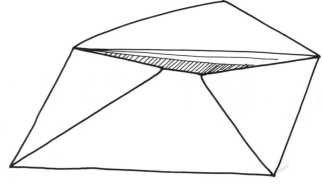

MATERIALS

For each set of four cards:

Four pieces of quality drawing paper or four blank note cards

Four envelopes to match the stationery

A selection of green leaves of different shapes and sizes—choose ones that have well-defined veins on the undersides

Printing inks or tempera paints

Shallow containers

Paintbrush

Paper towels

Scissors

Newspaper

PROCEDURE

1. Cover work area with newspaper.

2. Pour small amounts of paint or ink into the containers. If the paints are too thick, thin with water.

3. If you are using paper, help the child fold the paper in half, and cut to fit the envelopes.

4. Have the child put the leaf underside up on the newspaper. He or she should brush the leaf with paint or ink.

5. Have the child carefully lift up the painted leaf, and put it paint side down on the front of the folded paper or card. Cover with a clean paper towel.

6. Have the child press down on the paper towel firmly. Then lift off the towel and the leaf.

7. Repeat the process with the remaining cards. You might let children experiment with more than one leaf per card.

8. Allow cards to dry.

VARIATIONS

- Try painting the leaf more than one color.
- Use flowers or other natural objects that lie flat.

HELPFUL HINTS

For toddlers: You may have to help these children place the leaves on the cards and lift them off again. This will keep the paint from smearing and destroying the prints.

Dried Flower Cards

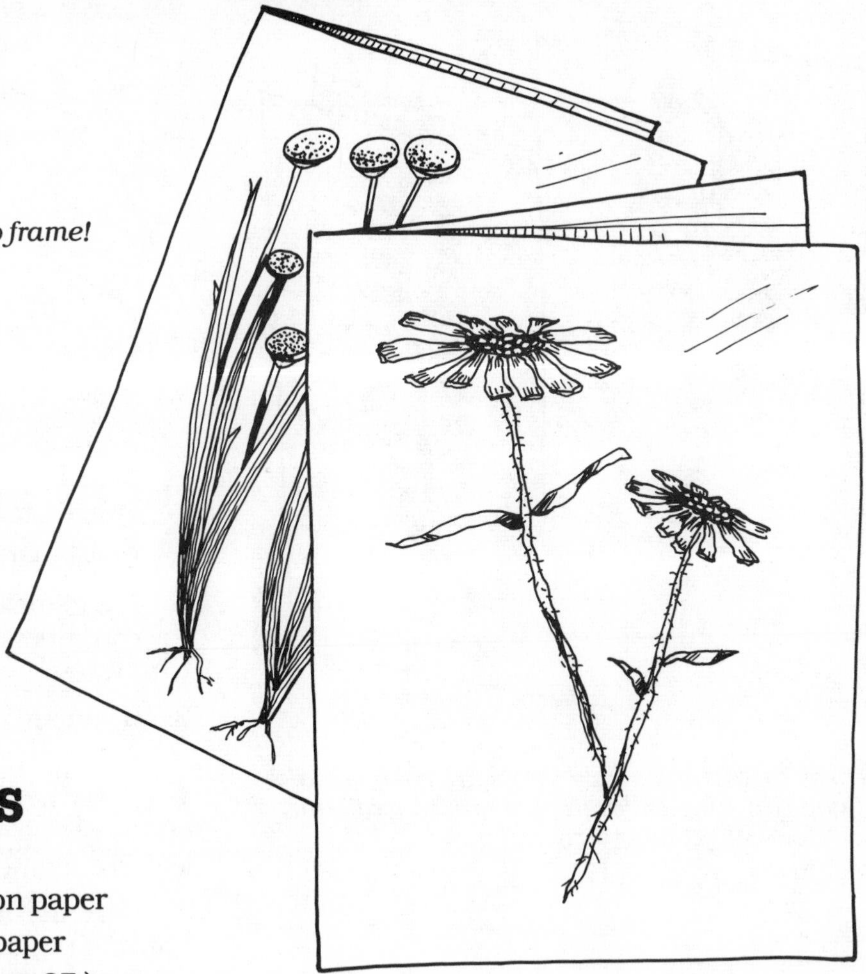

These cards are pretty enough to frame!

MATERIALS

For each card:

One 8½″ × 11″ piece construction paper
One 8½″ × 5½″ piece Con-Tact paper
Selection of dried flowers (See page 87.)
White glue
Glue brush

PROCEDURE

1.   Have the child fold the construction paper in half to 8½″ × 5½″.

2.   Have the child select several dried flowers to use on his or her card.

3.   Have the child carefully glue the flowers to the front of the card.

4.   Allow the glue to dry.

5.   Cover the front of the card with clear Con-Tact paper. Be careful not to break the flowers.

6.   Have the child dictate a message to write inside the card.

HELPFUL HINTS

For toddlers: This project is not recommended for this age group since the dried flowers are quite delicate.

For preschoolers: These children should be able to do most of the steps themselves. You might have them work with larger flowers, since the smaller the flower, the more fragile it is.

For primary grades: These children should be able to do this project with little assistance. You might suggest that they make patterns or scenes with the flowers.

Leaf-and-Crayon Place Mats

These place mats are a bit messy to make, but the results are terrific.

MATERIALS

For each place mat:

Two 9″ × 12″ pieces waxed paper

A selection of leaves of different shapes and sizes

Crayons

Newspaper

For teacher use:

Iron

PROCEDURE

1. Cover an area where you can use the iron with newspaper.

2. Have the child draw on one sheet of the waxed paper with crayons.

3. Have the child pick out several leaves to use in the place mat.

4. Have the child arrange the leaves on the colored waxed paper. Cover with the other sheet of waxed paper.

5. Place newspaper over the waxed paper and iron. (Have the child watch you during this step.)

6. Remove newspaper and let cool.

Flower Windows

A wonderful reminder of spring that looks nice in any window.

MATERIALS

For each window:

Waxed-paper sandwich bag
One 6″ piece yarn
A selection of leaves and flower petals
Newspaper

For teacher use:

Iron

PROCEDURE

1.   Cover an area where you can use the iron with newspaper.

2.   Have the child place several leaves and petals inside the sandwich bag. Make sure the plants do not overlap.

3.   Cover the sandwich bag with a sheet of newspaper and iron. (Have the child watch you during this step.)

4.   Remove the newspaper and let cool.

5.   Help the child punch two holes in the top of the bag, and tie the yarn through as a hanger.

VARIATIONS

•   Add bits of colored paper or crayon shavings before ironing the bag.

•   Make several flower windows and tape them together with black or silver tape for a "stained-glass" appearance.

Nature Walk Jars

Children love to save souvenirs from field trips. This beautiful gift will allow them to remember their trip for years to come.

MATERIALS

For each jar:

Glass jar with screw-on lid (Peanut butter jars are excellent.)

Handful of clay

Items from nature walk

PROCEDURE

1. Take the children on a nature walk. Have them collect dried plants, seeds, bark, twigs, and so on.

2. Help the child apply clay to the inside of the jar lid. Make sure there is enough clay to support the stems of the plants. Leave room so the jar can fit back on the lid.

3. Have each child arrange the plants and other items on the clay. Tell them to press the materials into the clay so they will stay.

4. Place the jar carefully over the arrangement and tighten it onto the lid.

5. Remind the child not to turn the jar right side up again.

VARIATION

*   Have children make figures out of clay to add to their arrangement.

HELPFUL HINTS

For toddlers and preschoolers: Younger children may have some problems remembering the dimensions of the jar. Make sure their arrangements will fit.

For primary grades: These children will probably need only minimal assistance. Encourage them to design a scene.

Potpourri Panels

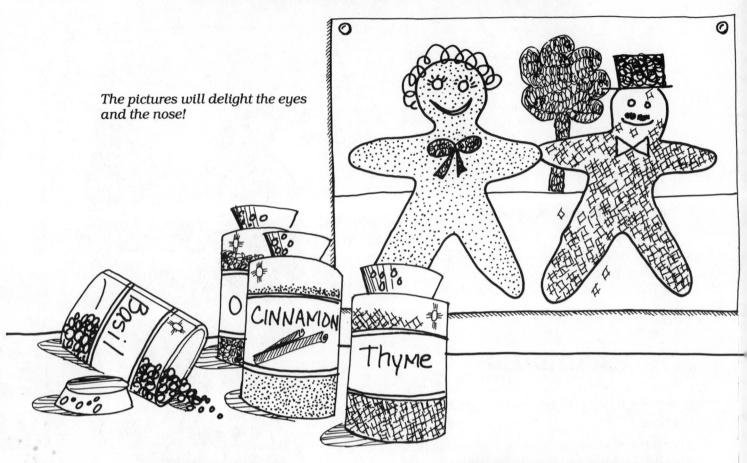

The pictures will delight the eyes and the nose!

MATERIALS

For each panel:

One 8½ × 11″ piece white posterboard

Variety of aromatic spices, such as thyme, mint, oregano, cinnamon, ginger, and basil

Permanent felt markers

White glue diluted with water

Glue brush

PROCEDURE

1. Have the child draw a picture on the posterboard with markers.

2. Have the child paint over portions of the picture with the glue.

3. Before the glue dries, have the child sprinkle different spices on the sticky areas. Allow to dry.

HELPFUL HINTS

For toddlers: Don't worry if these children don't paint the glue exactly over parts of their pictures. Allow them to experiment with the different spices.

For preschoolers: These children should be able to do this project with minimal assistance.

For primary grades: Encourage these children to make specific themes to fit the scents; for example, flowers, landscapes, or gingerbread people.

Walnut Shell Animals

These little creatures look nice decorating a shelf.

MATERIALS

For each animal:

Whole walnut or half a walnut shell

Tempera paints

Paintbrush

Decorating material or objects, such as construction paper, felt, and plastic eyes

Glue

Newspaper

PROCEDURE

1. Cover work area with newspaper.

2. Have the child paint the walnut shell. Allow to dry.

3. Have the child glue on features using the decorating materials. Allow to dry.

VARIATIONS

• Once the animal is done, have the child glue it to a piece of wood, which can serve as a stand. (This will provide an opportunity to experience the tactile sensations of wood.)

• Give children a variety of materials with which they can create the animals. For example, you might provide them with sticks, rocks, and other types of shells.

HELPFUL HINTS

For toddlers: Sometimes these children have problems gluing onto small areas. You might have them draw the features on the shell once the paint is dry.

Rock Paperweights

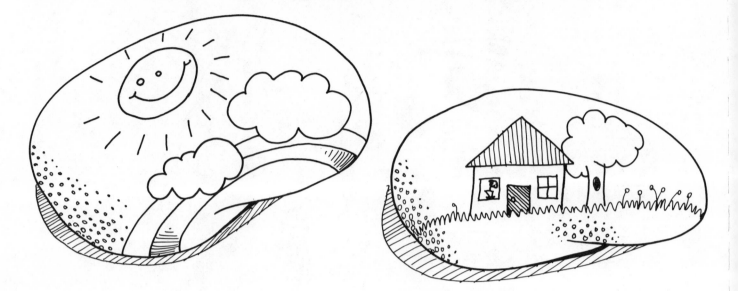

*Rocks are fun for children to decorate and are useful gifts—
they can become paperweights, bookends, and doorstops.*

MATERIALS

For each paperweight:

Smooth river rock (any size)

Tempera or enamel paints

Brush

Paper towels

Clear plastic spray

Newspaper

Glue (optional)

Felt or paper scraps (optional)

Plastic eyes (optional)

PROCEDURE

1. Cover work area with newspaper.

2. Help the child wash any dirt off the rock.
Dry with paper towels.

3. Have the child paint designs or animal
features on the rock. Allow to dry.

4. If you want, you can have the child
decorate the rock with pieces of felt or paper.
Allow the glue to dry.

5. Spray the rock with clear plastic. Allow
to dry.

HELPFUL HINTS

For toddlers and preschoolers: This age
group should use rocks that are large enough
to work as bookends or doorstops. You might
have children paint the rock one color and
then have them add accent colors.

For primary grades: You might have children combine several small rocks to make an
animal or creature. They should glue the rocks
together and allow the glue to dry before
painting.

Gifts from Odds and Ends

Napkin Rings

These napkin rings are attractive enough to enhance any festive table. For an extra-special gift include napkins in the rings.

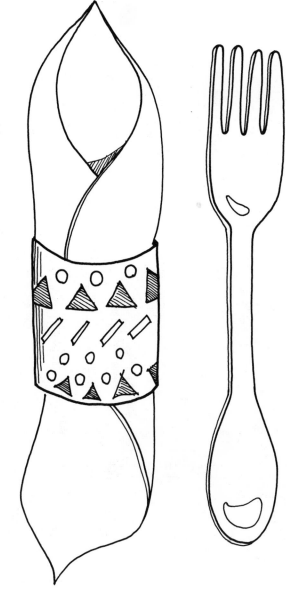

MATERIALS

For each set of five napkin rings:

One paper-towel roll

Five 3″ × 6″ pieces construction paper, foil, or fabric

Variety of decorating materials, such as tissue paper, lace, rickrack, fabric scraps, and construction paper

Glue

Scissors

PROCEDURE

1. Cut the paper-towel roll into five 2¼″ pieces of tube.

2. Have the child apply glue to a piece of tube. Make sure the outside is well covered.

3. Have the child roll a 3″ × 6″ piece of material around the tube. The material should be pressed tightly and held for a slow count of 15.

4. Have the child apply glue to the inside ends of the tube (about ½″ in). Help tuck in the ends of the material.

5. The child can decorate the tubes with any of the decorating materials. Allow the glue to dry.

HELPFUL HINTS

For toddlers and preschoolers: If you are using fabric or construction paper, you might have children use small scraps to cover the tube rather than one large piece. The smaller pieces will be easier for them to handle.

Bird Feeders

The sound and sight of chirping birds is the added bonus of this simple gift.

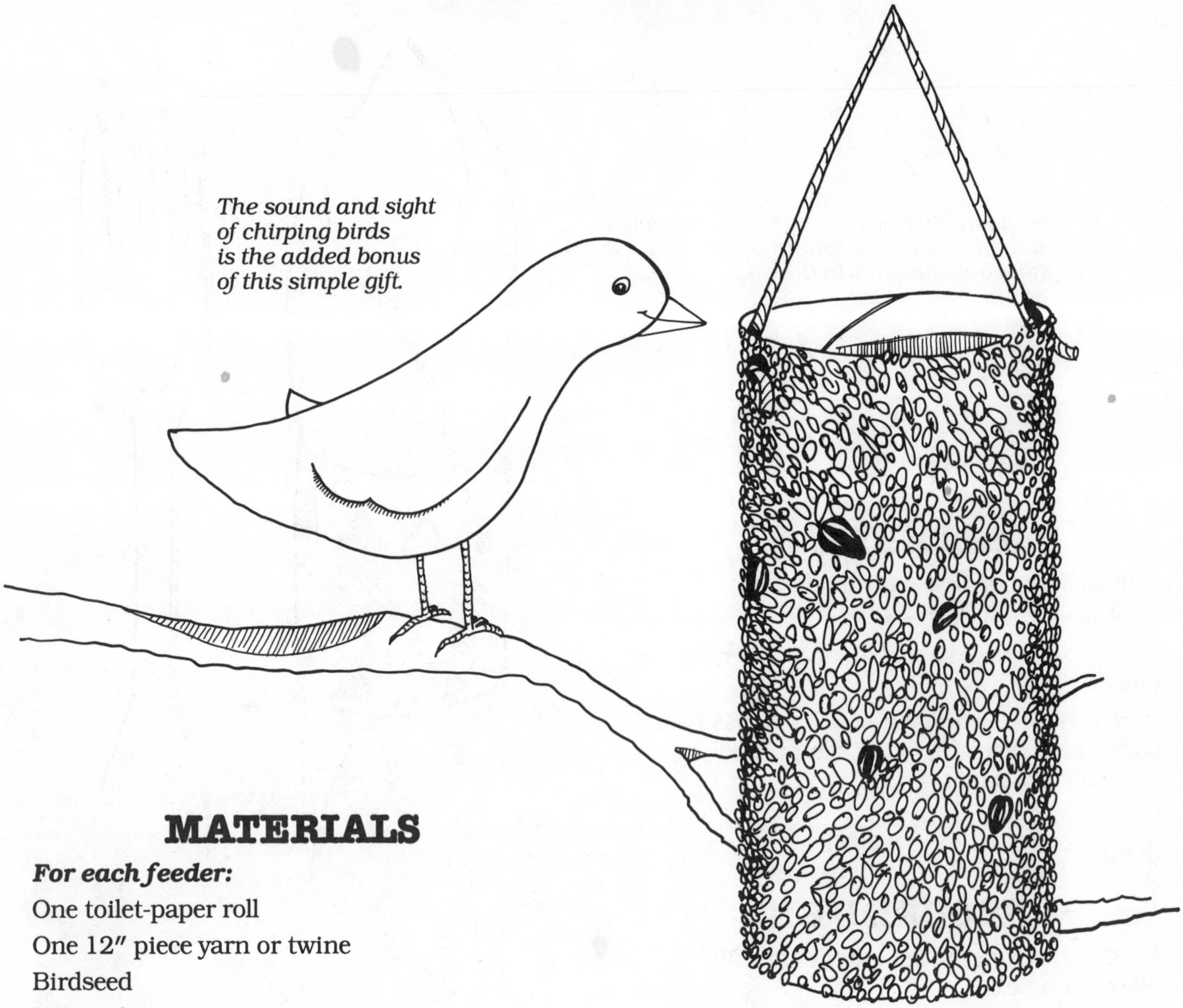

MATERIALS

For each feeder:

One toilet-paper roll

One 12″ piece yarn or twine

Birdseed

Peanut butter

Hole punch

Shallow pan with edges, such as a cookie sheet

PROCEDURE

1. Pour birdseed into pan. Let children smooth it out.

2. Help the child punch two holes in the top of the roll as shown.

3. Have the child smear peanut butter on the roll.

4. Have the child roll the feeder in the birdseed.

5. Help the child thread the yarn through the holes and tie a knot at the top. The bird feeder is now ready to hang.

VARIATION

• Try using pinecones instead of toilet-paper rolls.

Magazine-Picture Pencil Holders

A perfect Father's Day gift! Let children experiment with shapes, colors, and patterns when they make these delightful pencil holders.

MATERIALS

For each holder:

Frozen orange juice container

One piece clear Con-Tact paper

Collection of old magazines with color pictures

Scissors

White glue or glue stick

Glue brush

PROCEDURE

1. The child should find and cut out pictures from the magazines.

2. Help the child glue the magazine pictures to the orange juice can. Make sure the pictures cover the can.

3. Allow glue to dry.

4. Cover the can with clear Con-Tact paper. Trim the edges.

VARIATION

• You can substitute fabric, wallpaper, stamps, or almost anything that is made of cloth or paper for the magazine pictures. You might have children make seasonal pencil holders using wrapping paper.

HELPFUL HINTS

For toddlers: We prefer to use glue sticks with this age group—they are less messy and are easier for the children to use.

For primary grades: You might encourage children to make thematic holders.

Papier-mâché
Pencil Holders

Papier-mâché is one of those delightful gooey messes that everyone should have a chance to try. This is a fairly quick and simple project.

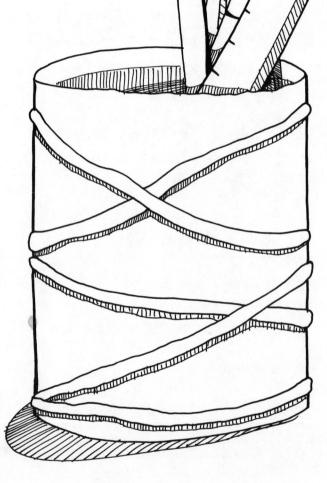

MATERIALS

For each holder:

One clean can, approximately soup-can size

Wheat paste or white glue

Old coffee cans or similar containers

Yarn

Newspaper

Tempera paints or spray paints

PROCEDURE

1. Mix the wheat paste with water until the mixture has the consistency of slightly runny oatmeal. If you prefer a mixture that is less gooey, use a combination of white glue and water instead.

2. Have the child tear the newspaper into strips that are less than 2″ wide.

3. The child should dip strips of newspaper into the wheat paste mixture and wipe off the excess as he or she pulls them out. Have the child apply the strips to the can by winding them around the can, keeping the strips as flat as possible. The child should continue until the can is covered.

4. Have the child dip some yarn in the paste mixture and wind it around the can for further decoration. Allow to dry for a day or two.

5. Have the child paint the can with tempera or spray paint.

HELPFUL HINTS

For primary grades: At this age, children can be creative with the yarn and paint. You might let them use a coat of varnish or watered-down glue as a finish.

Decorated Containers

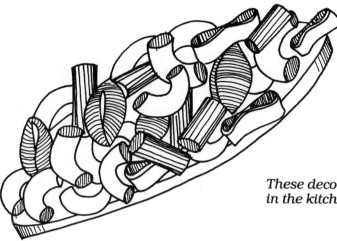

These decorative containers can be used in the kitchen, bedroom, or bathroom.

MATERIALS

For each container:

One coffee can with lid

Aluminum foil

Colored pasta shapes (See colored pasta recipe on page 86.)

Glue

Clear spray varnish (optional)

PROCEDURE

1. Have the child cover the outside of the coffee can with foil and glue it in place.

2. The child should decorate the lid by gluing pasta on top. Allow to dry.

3. If you want, spray varnish on the lid after the glue has dried.

VARIATIONS

• Have children use uncolored pasta and add beans and/or seeds.

• Have children paint the pasta with acrylic paint when the glue dries.

"Stained-Glass" Candle Holders

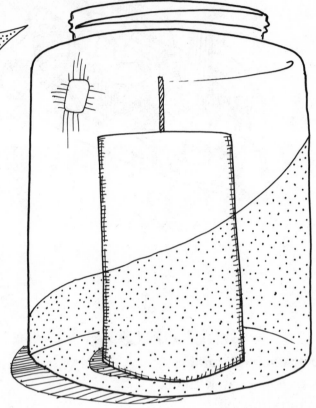

Create a colorful glow in any room with these brilliant candle holders.

MATERIALS

For each candle holder:

One baby-food jar, any size

One votive candle

Pieces of tissue paper, two or more colors

White glue

Scissors

Glue brush

Newspaper

PROCEDURE

1.   Cover work area with newspaper.

2.   Have the child cut or tear small pieces of tissue paper.

3.   Thin glue slightly with water so it spreads easily with a brush.

4.   Have the child glue the tissue paper pieces around the outside of the jar. The tissue pieces should overlap.

5.   Have the child apply another coat of glue. This will give the jar a varnished look when it is dry. Allow to dry.

6.   The child should put the candle in the jar. (If the jar has a small mouth, the candle should sit right on the top.) Now the gift is ready to give.

HELPFUL HINTS

For toddlers: Toddlers will probably need precut shapes and help with spreading the glue.

For preschoolers: These children should be able to complete the project with adult supervision. You might have them cut out tissue paper shapes, such as circles, triangles, and rectangles.

For primary grades: Encourage children to develop patterns as they place tissue shapes on the jar.

Sock Puppets

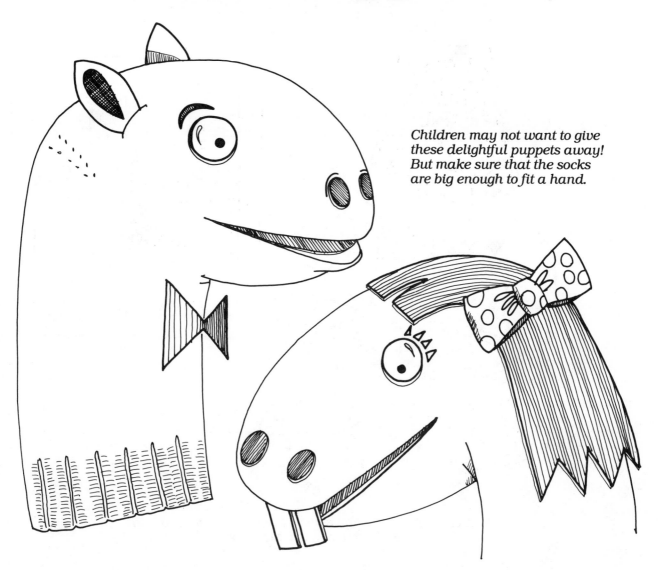

Children may not want to give these delightful puppets away! But make sure that the socks are big enough to fit a hand.

MATERIALS

For each puppet:

One old sock

Cloth scraps

Felt scraps

Cardboard

Glue

Scissors

Plastic eyes (optional)

FIGURE A

PROCEDURE

1. Have each child stuff the toe of the sock with fabric scraps.

2. Cut a piece of cardboard as shown (see Figure A). Then have the child fold the cardboard piece in half and glue it to the instep of the sock.

3. Have the child glue on eyes and other decorations cut out of felt.

HELPFUL HINTS

For toddlers: These children will be able to stuff the sock and add decorations, but you may have to help them glue in the cardboard mouth.

Paper Plate Tambourines

*Children might want to give these tambourines to a sibling,
just so they can use them, too.*

MATERIALS

For each tambourine:

Two paper plates

Kidney beans or any other large beans

Felt pens

Tape

PROCEDURE

1. Have the child decorate the backs of the plates with felt pens.

2. Have the child turn one of the plates right side up and place 10–20 beans on the plate.

3. Have the child place the second plate upside down over the first plate.

4. Help the child tape the plates together.

HELPFUL HINTS

For primary grades: You might have the children punch holes in the plates and sew the plates together rather than taping them together.

Pot-Holder Holders

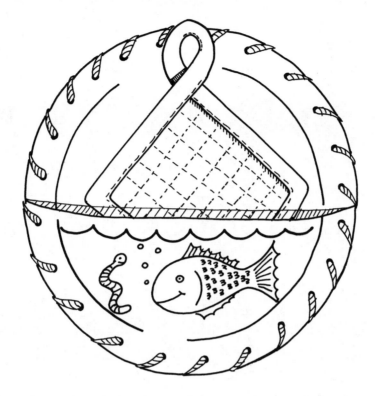

This useful gift is easy to make and lasts a long time.

MATERIALS

For each pot-holder holder:

Two paper plates

Large-eye blunt needle

One 30″ piece yarn

Felt pens or crayons

Scissors

Hole punch

PROCEDURE

1. Have the child fold one of the plates in half.

2. The child should unfold the plate and cut along the crease. Have the child discard one of the halves.

3. Have the child put the whole paper plate and the half paper plate together. Help the child punch holes as shown in Figure A.

4. Thread the needle for the child and tie a knot in one end of the yarn.

5. Have the child put the plates together again, this time with the front sides of the plates facing each other. Make sure the holes are aligned.

6. Have the child sew the two plates together starting at the top and using an overlapping stitch (see Figure B).

7. Help the child tie the ends of the yarn together to make a hanger.

8. Have the child decorate the holder with felt pens or crayons.

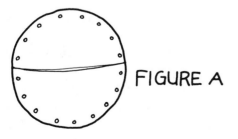

FIGURE A

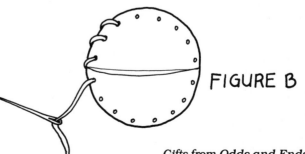

FIGURE B

Pasta Plaques

These mosaic plaques would look nice hanging in a kitchen.

MATERIALS

For each plaque:

One Styrofoam tray, such as a meat tray

Pasta in assorted shapes and sizes

Yarn

White glue

Paint (optional)

Paintbrush (optional)

PROCEDURE

1.   Have each child squeeze a line of glue in a simple scribble shape on the tray.

2.   Have the child place yarn on the tray, following the glue line.

3.   Have the child make a mosaic by gluing a different kind of pasta into each section formed by the yarn. Allow glue to dry.

4.   Have children paint the noodles or cover them with a thin layer of glue to create a shiny finish. Let dry.

VARIATIONS

•   Use colored pasta (See colored pasta recipe on page 86.)

•   Substitute beans and/or seeds for the pasta.

•   Substitute a piece of wood for the Styrofoam tray.

HELPFUL HINTS

For toddlers: These children might have some problems working with very small pieces of pasta and filling in small areas. You might want to create the yarn design for them and have them use macaroni wheels or rigatoni to fill in the spaces.

For preschoolers: Encourage these children to make simple designs. They might need help placing the yarn directly on the glue lines.

For primary grades: These children can complete this activity with minimal supervision. You might encourage them to create patterns within each yarn section.

Mix and Measure Gifts

Bubble Bath

This is an ideal activity for children who are beginning to measure. The recipe does not require a great deal of accuracy for the project to be successful.

MATERIALS

For each cup of bubble bath:

One 10-ounce container with lid (You shouldn't use glass containers for this project.)

One index card

Baby oil or safflower oil

Mild scented shampoo

Water

Measuring cups and spoons

Stickers

Tape

PROCEDURE

1. Have the child combine the following in the container.

   6 teaspoons oil

   ½ cup shampoo

   ½ cup water

2. Have the child cover the container with the lid and shake it.

3. Allow the child to decorate the container with stickers.

4. Write the following directions on the index card, and have each child attach the card to the container.

Add several tablespoons of bubble bath to warm bath water. Sit back and enjoy.

HELPFUL HINTS

For toddlers: You might want to measure the ingredients, and then have the child pour them into the container. Children can complete this gift by shaking and decorating the container. Be sure to watch out for soap in the eyes.

For preschoolers: These children will have fun measuring the ingredients, but they will need assistance securing the lid and writing the instructions.

For primary grades: This is an ideal activity for this age group, since only minimal supervision is necessary.

Handmade Soap Balls

This gift can be decoratively wrapped in a seashell, basket, or a box, and given with the bubble bath (page 49) as a gift set.

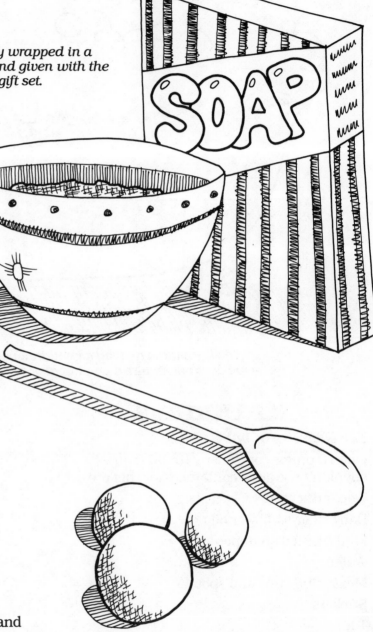

MATERIALS

For 20–30 soap balls:

Four cups soap flakes

One-half cup water

One-half teaspoon food coloring

Mixing bowl

Measuring cups and spoons

Large spoon

Cookie sheet

Foil

PROCEDURE

1. Have children measure the soap flakes and put them in the mixing bowl.

2. Have children add the food coloring to the soap.

3. Help the children add small amounts of water. Stir until the soap pulls away from the sides of the bowl and forms a ball. The mixture should be thick but not sticky.

4. Give each child a small amount of the soap mixture (about 1–2 teaspoons).

5. Have the child roll the soap into a ball using the palms of his or her hands.

6. Have the children place the finished soap balls on a foil-covered cookie sheet.

7. Allow the soap balls to dry for about a week.

HELPFUL HINTS

For toddlers: These children can pour the ingredients after you measure them. Don't worry if they can't form perfect balls—the hand process is difficult for this age group.

Plaster Paperweights

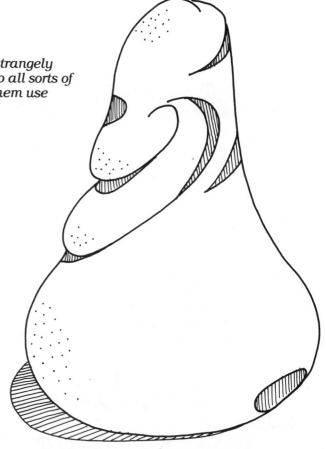

Children can turn these strangely shaped paperweights into all sorts of creatures or objects. Let them use their imaginations!

MATERIALS

For each paperweight:

One plastic cup

One plastic spoon

One plastic bag (large sandwich size)

Plaster of paris

Water

Tempera

Paintbrush

Clear varnish

PROCEDURE

1. Have each child mix the following together in the plastic cup:

      4 tablespoons plaster of paris
      2 tablespoons water

2. Have the child stir the mixture well.

3. Help the child pour the mixture into the corner of a plastic bag. Have the child twist the top of the bag. Let the bag sit for about two minutes until the plaster begins to set.

4. Have the child twist the bag and the plaster into strange shapes. When the child is satisfied with the shape, let the bag sit for about half an hour or until the plaster is completely set.

5. Remove the sculpture from the bag and have the child paint it with tempera. Allow to dry.

6. If you wish, you can have the child varnish the paperweight.

HELPFUL HINTS

For toddlers: You may need to assist these children with the measuring. They can pour the plaster and water into the cup and help stir.

Dough Bead Necklaces

MATERIALS

For each necklace:

One 18″ piece yarn

Large-eye blunt needle

Small container for mixing dough

Flour

Salt

Water

Foil

Measuring spoons

Tempera paints (optional)

Paintbrush (optional)

This project gives the child a chance to squeeze, pound, roll, pinch, and create freely.

PROCEDURE

1.   Have each child mix the following in the container:

> 8 tablespoons flour
> 4 tablespoons salt

2.   Have the child add 4 tablespoons water.

3.   Have the child stir the mixture well. Check to see whether he or she needs to add more water or flour. The resulting dough should form a nonsticky ball.

4.   Have the child pinch off pieces of the baker's clay and roll them into balls.

5.   Have the child string the beads by pushing the needle and yarn gently through the center of the balls.

6.   When the string of beads is finished it should be placed on foil and allowed to dry for several days. Have the child turn the string occasionally so the beads dry evenly on all sides.

7.   When the beads are thoroughly dry they can be painted, or worn as is.

Dough Art Candle Holders

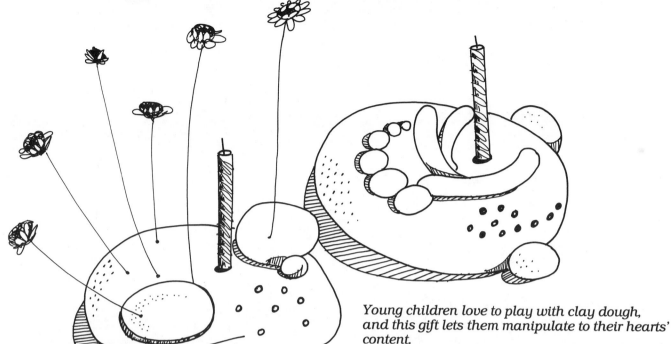

Young children love to play with clay dough, and this gift lets them manipulate to their hearts' content.

MATERIALS

For each candle holder:

Flour

Salt

Water

Small container for mixing dough

Foil

Measuring cups

Assortment of decorating items, such as twigs, whole cloves, peppercorns, buttons, and straw flowers

Birthday cake candle

Food coloring

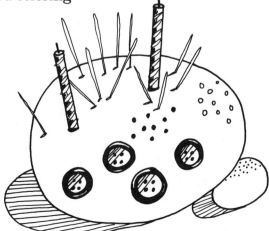

PROCEDURE

1. Have each child mix the following in the container:

    ½ cup flour
    ¼ cup salt

2. Have the child add:

    ¼ cup water
    several drops food coloring

3. Have the child stir the mixture well. Check to see whether he or she needs to add more water or flour. The resulting dough should form a nonsticky ball.

4. Have the child model the candle holder on the piece of foil. The decorating items and candle may be stuck into the clay while it is being modeled.

5. Allow to dry for several days.

VARIATION

• Have the child make uncolored clay. When the child is finished with the candle holder, remove the candle and bake at 300 or 325 degrees for several hours. This will give the clay a golden color. The child can glue the candle back in place when the piece is cooled.

Sand Candle Holders

This gift is inexpensive, useful, and beautiful to look at.

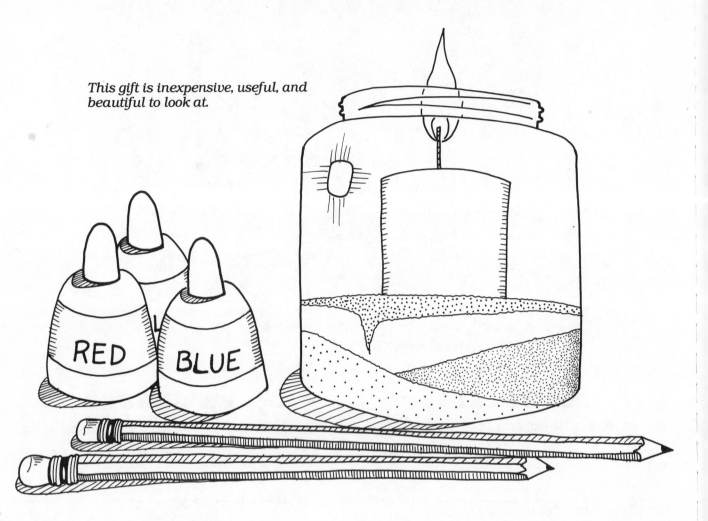

MATERIALS

For each candle holder:

Wide-mouth baby-food jar

One votive candle

Terrarium sand

Containers with lids

Food coloring

Pencils

Paraffin wax

For teacher use:

Small pot for melting wax

Hot plate or stove

PROCEDURE

1.   Have children make colored sand. (See recipe on page 86.)

2.   Have each child pour small amounts of different colors of sand into the jar. You should be able to see several different layers of sand. The child can use a pencil to make indentations and form a landscape in the sand.

3.   Melt the wax in the pot.

4.   Pour a thin coat of melted wax over the completed sand pattern. This would be a good time to discuss safety.

5.   Help the child place the votive candle on top of the melted wax.

6.   Allow wax to cool.

VARIATION

- Use colored sugar instead of colored sand.

Peanut Butter Thumbprint Candy

Children love to make this tasty gift!

MATERIALS

For 12 pieces of candy:

One cup peanut butter

One cup honey

One and a half cups powdered milk

Mixing bowl

Large spoon

Measuring cups

Cookie sheet

PROCEDURE

1. Have children measure the peanut butter and the honey into the bowl.

2. Let children stir the mixture until it is well combined.

3. Have children add powdered milk. Mix well.

4. Let children roll teaspoon amounts of the dough into balls. They should set these on the cookie tray.

5. Have children press a thumb into the center of the peanut butter balls to form a print.

6. Refrigerate before serving or packaging.

Snowballs

These pretty coconut balls should be given the day they're made.

MATERIALS

For each batch of snowballs:

Six ounces softened cream cheese

Five cups powdered sugar

One-half teaspoon vanilla

One bag of coconut flakes

Mixing bowl

Large spoon

Measuring cups and spoons

Cookie sheet

PROCEDURE

1. Have children measure the sugar into the bowl, and add the cream cheese.

2. Let children stir the mixture until it is smooth.

3. Have children add the vanilla. Mix well.

4. Let children roll teaspoon amounts of the mixture into balls.

5. Spread the coconut on the cookie sheet.

6. Have children roll the cream cheese balls in the coconut.

7. Refrigerate before serving or packaging.

VARIATION

- Use food coloring to dye the coconut and have the children make multicolored balls.

Holiday Gifts and Decorations

Reindeer Decorations

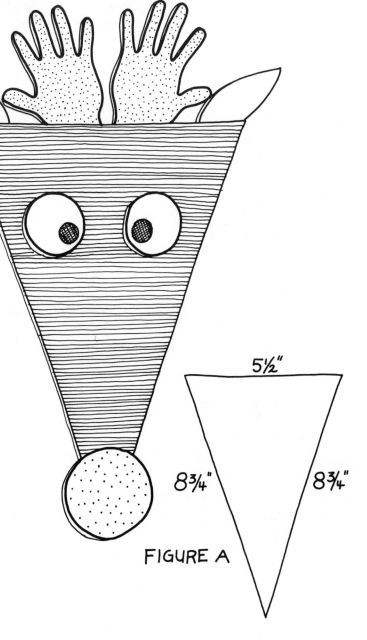

This is a fun holiday gift or decoration for all ages to make.

MATERIALS

For each reindeer:

Two 9″ × 12″ pieces felt or brown construction paper

Scraps of various-colored felt or construction paper

Black felt pen or white chalk

Scissors

Glue

Heavy paper or posterboard

PROCEDURE

1.   Draw a triangle on the heavy paper or posterboard. (Use the dimensions shown in Figure A.) Cut out the triangle.

2.   Have the child trace the triangle pattern on one piece of the felt or paper. Help the child cut out the triangle if necessary.

3.   Have the child place his or her palm on the second piece of felt or paper, and spread his or her fingers. Trace around the hand using the felt pen or chalk.

4.   Repeat the process with the child's other hand. These will be the reindeer's antlers. Help the child cut out the handprints.

5. Have the child cut out small ears from the remaining scraps. The child should also cut out a small red circle for a nose, and two more circles for eyes.

6.   Have the child glue the antlers, ears, nose, and eyes onto the triangle as shown. Allow to dry.

7.   Help the child add small thread loops to antlers for hangers.

5½″

8¾″

8¾″

FIGURE A

HELPFUL HINTS

For toddlers: With this age group, this project will be essentially adult directed. These children will enjoy the gluing and the final results. You might use the project to discuss the parts of the face and the position of those parts.

For preschoolers: These children will be able to draw and cut the reindeer parts from paper, but will probably need help cutting felt. If possible the children should do their own cutting—the little imperfections make each reindeer unique.

Original Art Christmas Ornaments

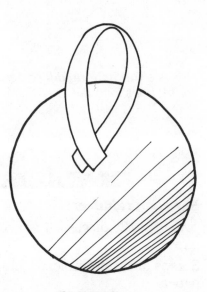

Children love to hang ornaments on a tree, especially when they've made them!

FIGURE A

MATERIALS

For each ornament:

One metal jar lid, such as a mayonnaise jar lid or a peanut-butter jar lid

One 8½″ × 11″ piece construction paper

One 7″–8″ piece ribbon or yarn

Fine-tip felt pens

An assortment of decorating material, such as yarn, lace, or trim

Glue

Scissors

Cotton balls (optional)

PROCEDURE

1. Have the child trace the lid twice on the paper.

2. Have the child cut out the circles. Then trim one of the circles so it fits inside the lid.

3. Have the child draw a Christmas or winter scene on the smaller circle.

4. Have the child glue the circle to the inside of the lid.

5. Make a loop out of the ribbon and glue to the back of the lid. (See Figure A.)

6. Write the child's name and the year on the large circle. Have him or her glue the large circle to the back of the lid, over the ribbon.

7. Have the child decorate the outside of the lid with scraps of yarn, lace, or trim. For a "snowy" effect, add pieces of cotton to the picture.

VARIATION

• Substitute circles cut out from old Christmas cards or wrapping paper for the construction paper circles.

HELPFUL HINTS

For toddlers: Have children draw on a large piece of paper. Then cut out the circles from this paper. If you are using Christmas cards or wrapping paper, toddlers can choose the pictures to use, and glue them once they have been cut.

For preschoolers: You can simplify this project by giving the children precut circles.

For primary grades: This project was originally developed for this age group. They have little or no trouble completing the project themselves.

Glitter Ornaments

Stars, moons, diamonds, and other shapes can be used to make these sparkling treasures for a special person's Christmas tree.

MATERIALS

For each ornament:

Precut ornament (See patterns on page 90.)

Ornament hanger or paper clip

Glitter (assorted colors)

Pie pan

Posterboard

Scissors

Glue

Glue brush

Hole punch

PROCEDURE

1.   Before class use the ornament patterns to trace a variety of shapes on the posterboard. Cut out.

2.   Have each child pick a precut ornament.

3.   Help the child punch a hole in the top of the ornament. This is the hanger hole.

4.   Have the child spread glue on one side of the shape.

5.   Have the child sprinkle the shape with glitter. This process should be done over a pie pan to catch the excess glitter. Allow to dry.

6.   Repeat the process for the second side. Insert hanger and let hang until dry.

HELPFUL HINTS

For preschoolers and primary grades: If children can cut posterboard and trace, allow them to cut out their own ornaments. They may also wish to design their own shapes to use.

Geometric String Ornaments

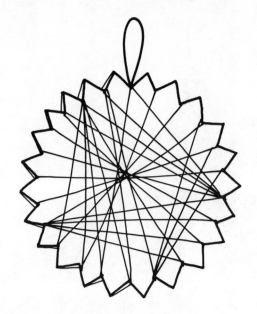

This project is great for children who have trouble waiting! It's quick, easy, and can be hung on a tree immediately.

MATERIALS

For each ornament:

Precut ornament (See step 1 of procedure.)

Ornament hanger or paper clip

Posterboard

Pinking shears

Embroidery thread, yarn, or colored string

PROCEDURE

1. Before class trace a circle for each child on posterboard, and cut out with pinking shears.

2. Cut a ¼″ slit into the circle. Help the child tie a knot in the thread, and anchor in the slit as shown (see Figure A).

3. Have the child wrap the thread around the circle, catching it in the Vs formed by the pinking shears. This will form a design.

4. Help the child tie a knot to hold the thread in place when the ornament is finished.

5. Add an ornament hanger and it's ready to hang!

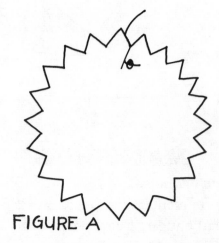

FIGURE A

VARIATION

• When the design is finished, spray it with spray glue and add a small amount of glitter.

HELPFUL HINTS

For primary grades: Older children should be able to cut out their own circles. In fact, they may want to try varying the size of the circle, or making several circles that they can attach to make a chain.

Hanukkah Dreidels

A wonderful toy to give and to receive. These are simple and inexpensive gifts to make.

MATERIALS

For each dreidel:

Small milk or cream carton (pint size)

Sharpened pencil

Tape

Tempera paints

Paintbrush

Newspaper

PROCEDURE

1. Cover the work area with newspaper.

2. Help the child tape down the tops of the milk carton to make a box.

3. Have the child paint the box.

4. Let the box dry.

5. Help the child poke a pencil through the box.

HELPFUL HINTS

For toddlers: These children will be able to paint the boxes, but you will have to tape the tops down and poke the pencil through.

For preschoolers: These children should be able to do this activity with minimal assistance.

For primary grades: You might have these children paint a different scene or figure on each side of the box.

Valentine Puzzle Cards

This is an unusual way to say "I love you."

MATERIALS

For each card:

One 8½″ × 11″ piece of red or white construction paper

One standard-size envelope

Posterboard

Felt pens

Scissors

Pencil

PROCEDURE

1. Trace a heart on posterboard and cut out.

2. Have each child trace around the posterboard heart on the construction paper.

3. Help the child write a message on the heart.

4. Have the child draw lines on the heart to form puzzle pieces. Then cut along the lines.

5. Have the child put the puzzle pieces in the envelope. Be sure to include directions to the receiver of the card; for example, "Put the pieces together to receive my Valentine message."

HELPFUL HINTS

For toddlers and preschoolers: These children can assist with the tracing and the cutting. Small children can dictate a message for you to write on the heart.

Valentine Rubbing Cards

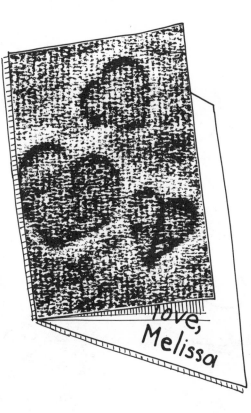

*Children love to watch the hearts
appear on their paper as if by magic!*

MATERIALS

For each card:

Two 8½″ × 11″ pieces white paper

Crayons

Paper clips

Paper or cardboard hearts in a variety of sizes

PROCEDURE

1. Have the child pick out several hearts to use on his or her card.

2. Have the child put the hearts on one sheet of paper and place the other sheet on top.

3. Help clip the sheets together to keep them from slipping.

4. Have the child rub the side of the crayon over the surface of the paper. The hearts will appear on the sheet.

5. Have the child unclip the sheets and fold the rubbing in half.

6. Help the child write a message inside the card.

VARIATION

• Use different shapes, such as Christmas trees, four-leaf clovers, or pumpkins, to adapt these cards for other holidays.

Decorated Eggs

*These imaginative eggs are a treat
for anyone to receive.*

MATERIALS

For each egg:

One raw egg

Safety pin

Water-soluble egg dye

Crayons

Bowl

PROCEDURE

1. Poke a small hole in the top and bottom of the egg using the safety pin.

2. Have the child hold the egg over the bowl and blow as hard as possible into the hole. This will force the yolk and white out through the other end.

3. Rinse the eggshell and let it dry.

4. Have the child draw on the eggshell with the crayons, being careful to leave some white space.

5. Prepare egg dye and have the child dye the egg.

6. Allow the egg to dry.

HELPFUL HINTS

For toddlers: This project is not recommended for this age group.

For preschoolers: You may have to help these children blow their eggs clean. You should also caution them to draw lightly on the egg.

For primary grades: These children should be able to do this project with minimal supervision.

Easter Chicks

Combine these chicks with the Easter eggs for a delightful Easter basket.

MATERIALS

For each chick:

One segment of an egg-carton bottom

Two cotton balls

Scraps of yellow, red, and black construction paper

Easter-egg grass

Glue

Felt pens

PROCEDURE

1. Have the child glue a small amount of Easter-egg grass inside the egg-carton segment.

2. Have the child glue the two cotton balls together.

3. Have the child make a tiny face on one of the cotton balls using small scraps of construction paper.

4. Have the child put the chick inside the "egg."

5. Let the child decorate the outside of the egg with felt pens.

Folded-Paper Baskets

This basket is great for holding Easter Chicks and Decorated Eggs.

MATERIALS

For each basket:

One 9″ × 12″ piece construction paper

One 3″ × 12″ piece construction paper

Glue or glue stick

Scissors

Felt pens

Stickers (optional)

PROCEDURE

1.   Help the child fold the 9″ × 12″ piece of construction paper into thirds lengthwise. Then unfold the paper.

2.   Help the child fold the paper into thirds widthwise. Unfold the paper again.

3.   Have the child cut along the folds as shown in Figure A.

4.   Help the child fold corner A and corner B together until the tips of the corners just meet (see Figure B). Make sure flap C stays outside the fold. Glue together.

5.   Repeat on the opposite side.

6.   Have the child form a handle by folding the 3″ × 12″ paper into thirds lengthwise. Have the child glue the edges together and let it dry.

7.   Help the child glue the handle to the sides of the basket (see Figure C).

8.   Help the child glue flap C over the handle. This helps hold the handle in place.

9.   Have the child decorate the basket with felt pens. You might also use stickers for decoration.

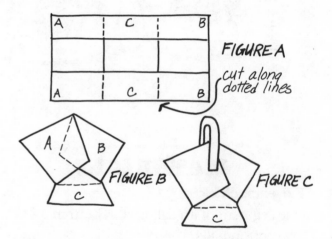

FIGURE A
cut along dotted lines

FIGURE B

FIGURE C

HELPFUL HINTS

For toddlers: Have young children draw on the paper *before* you start to cut and form the baskets. You will probably have to do most of the assembly yourself.

For preschoolers: This is a good project for scissor practice. Children get positive results even if the cutting is slightly crooked. These children will need some help with assembling the basket.

For primary grades: It is helpful to make a sample basket before having these children work on their own. You might label the paper for the children before they cut it so that construction will be easier.

Stuffed Pumpkins

*An easy and quick way
to have pumpkins for Halloween.*

MATERIALS

For each pumpkin:

Small paper bag

Newspaper

Masking tape

Poster paint

Paintbrush

Black construction paper

Scissors

PROCEDURE

1. Have the child stuff the paper bag with crumpled newspaper.

2. Help the child twist the bag shut. Wrap tape around the twisted end to make a stem.

3. Have the child paint the bag orange, and add details to make a pumpkin.

4. Help the child cut facial features out of the paper and stick them on the pumpkin before the paint dries.

Halloween Creatures

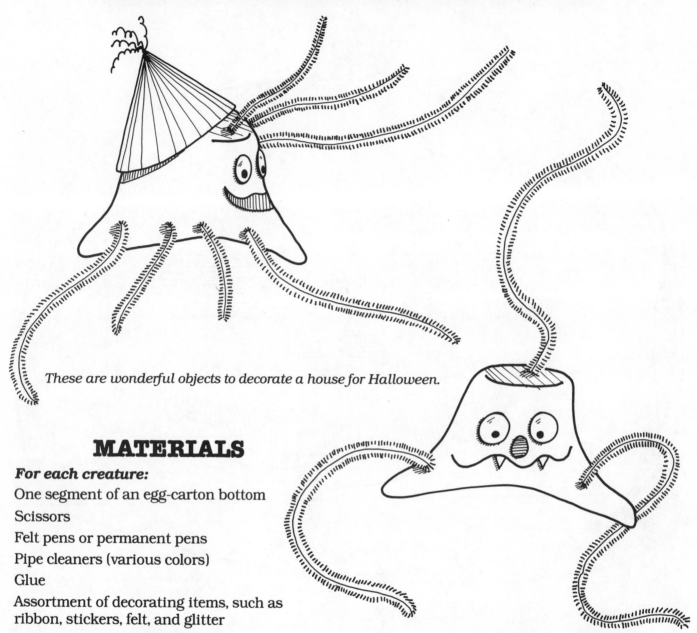

These are wonderful objects to decorate a house for Halloween.

MATERIALS

For each creature:

One segment of an egg-carton bottom

Scissors

Felt pens or permanent pens

Pipe cleaners (various colors)

Glue

Assortment of decorating items, such as ribbon, stickers, felt, and glitter

PROCEDURE

1. Have the child draw a face on the egg-carton segment. (If you are using Styrofoam sections, you should provide permanent pens.)

2. The child can use pipe cleaners as legs.

3. Let the child decorate his or her creature with the other materials.

VARIATION

•   Give the children several egg-carton segments and let them build a creature. They can glue the pieces together in numerous different shapes, such as a caterpillar or a creature from Mars. You might let older children write stories about their creatures.

Creative Wrapping Papers

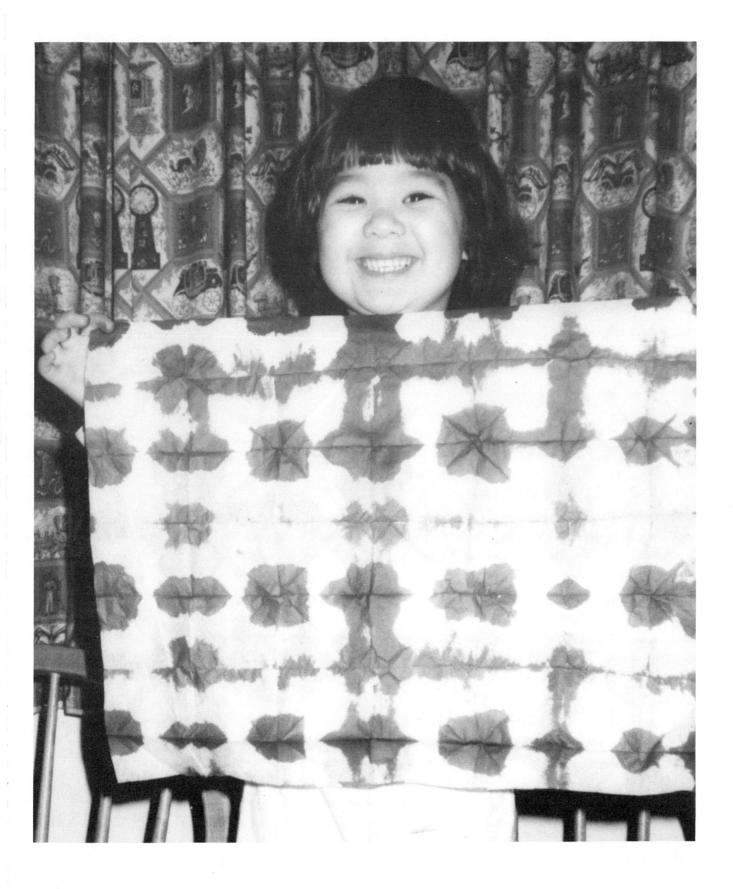

Sponge-Stamp Wrapping Paper

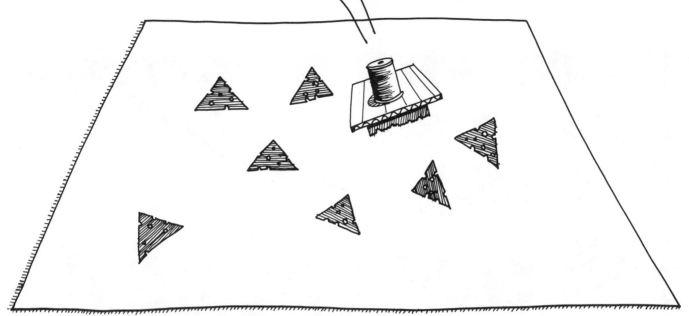

Bright and wonderful wrapping paper is fun to make in large pieces.
Lay the paper on a long table and let the children go wild with the stamps.

MATERIALS

For each stamp:

One 3″ × 5″ sponge (½″ thick)

One 3″ × 5″ piece corrugated cardboard

Empty spool

Scissors

Rubber cement

Felt pen

For each piece of wrapping paper:

One 9″ × 12″ or larger piece butcher paper, tissue paper, or shelf paper

Tempera paints

Flat-bottom containers for paint

Newspaper

PROCEDURE

1. Cover work area with newspaper.

2. Have each child draw a simple design on a sponge.

3. Cut out the sponge shape.

4. Have the child glue the sponge shape to the cardboard and allow it to dry.

5. Have the child glue the spool to the top of the cardboard. This will be the handle. Allow to dry.

6. Check consistency of the paint. You should be able to reproduce the exact shape of the stamp without the paint running. Thin paint with water if necessary.

7. Have the child dip the sponge in the paint and print the wrapping paper by pressing the sponge down firmly on the paper.

8. The child should repeat the process until he or she is pleased with the design. You might suggest using different colors or stamps.

HELPFUL HINTS

For toddlers: You will have to make the stamps for this age group.

For preschoolers: Preschoolers should be able to help with the stamp design and the gluing, but you should do the cutting.

Vegetable-Stamp Wrapping Paper

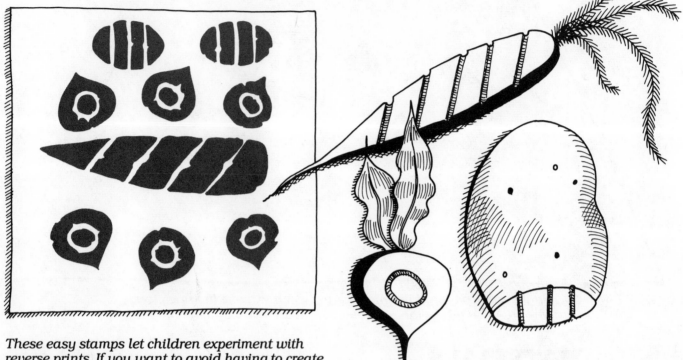

These easy stamps let children experiment with reverse prints. If you want to avoid having to create a pattern, try vegetables or fruits with inherent patterns, such as celery or oranges.

MATERIALS

For each stamp:

A vegetable, such as a potato, a carrot, or a turnip

Knife

For each piece of wrapping paper:

One 9″ × 12″ or larger piece butcher paper, tissue paper, or shelf paper

Tempera paints or stamp pads (See homemade stamp pad recipe on page 85.)

Flat bottom container

Paintbrush

Newspaper

PROCEDURE

1. Cover work area with newspaper.

2. Cut the vegetables in half.

3. Cut a pattern across the open surface of the vegetable. Remember that the area you do not cut will be the area that will print.

4. Have children brush paint over the cut surface, or press the stamp onto a stamp pad.

5. Have children print by pressing the piece of vegetable firmly on the paper.

6. When the paint is dry, the paper is ready to use.

VARIATION

•   Try using pieces of fruit instead of vegetables.

HELPFUL HINTS

For primary grades: These children can help you cut the vegetables. They can also be encouraged to develop patterns with their stamping.

Cardboard-Block Wrapping Paper

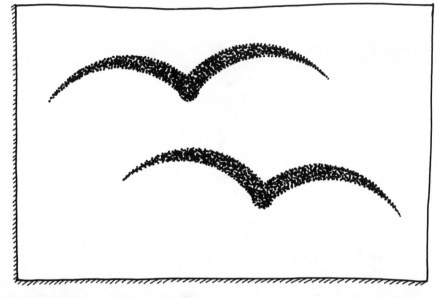

This project can easily be adapted for any age group. Older children can make the stamps and use them, while younger children can use stamps that have already been made.

MATERIALS

For each stamp:

Heavy cardboard

Scissors or razor blade

Glue

For each piece of wrapping paper:

One 8½″ × 11″ or larger piece shelf or butcher paper

Tempera paints

Paintbrush

Tape

Newspaper

PROCEDURE

1. Before class cut out several simple shapes from the cardboard. You might pick theme patterns, such as pumpkins, four-leaf clovers, or neckties, or use the sample patterns on page 90. Glue the shape to a larger piece of cardboard to make the block. Let it dry.

2. Cover the work area with newspaper.

3. Have the child place a cardboard block on the work area and tape it down.

4. Have the child paint the raised cardboard section.

5. Have the child place the paper on top of the paint-covered block and gently rub the paper. The child should slowly pick up the paper to reveal the print.

6. Repeat the process so the design is printed on several areas of the paper. Let dry.

7. If you need to change colors on the same block, wipe the block clean with a paper towel while the paint is still wet.

HELPFUL HINTS

For toddlers and preschoolers: You might consider substituting construction paper for the shelf or butcher paper. Have the child make one print that can be cut out and glued to the top of a present wrapped in tissue paper.

For primary grades: You might have these children experiment with multicolored prints. They can make these by painting the block several different colors.

Wheel-Track Wrapping Paper

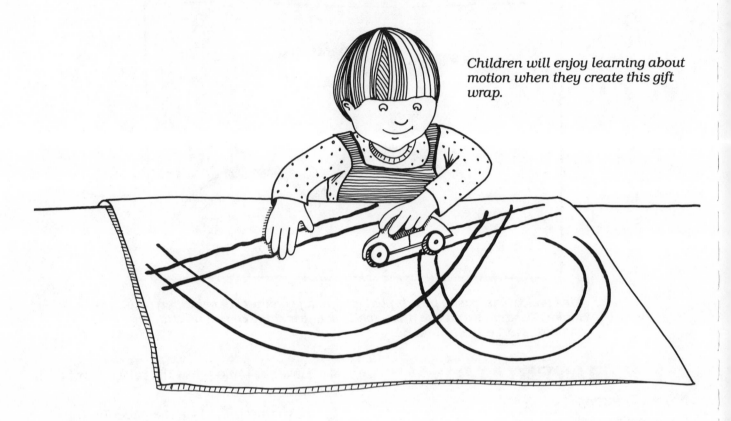

Children will enjoy learning about motion when they create this gift wrap.

MATERIALS

For each piece of wrapping paper:

One 9″ × 12″ piece shelf paper or butcher paper

Small toy cars, trucks, or airplanes

Liquid tempera paints

Shallow trays

Newspaper

PROCEDURE

1. Cover the work area with newspaper.

2. Pour a small amount of the tempera into the trays.

3. Have the child dip the wheels of the vehicle in the paint.

4. The child should drive the vehicle across the paper to make paint tracks.

5. Continue until the child is satisfied with the design. Allow to dry.

HELPFUL HINTS

For toddlers and preschoolers: Most young children really love this activity. You might provide them with long strips of paper.

For primary grades: You might encourage children to create stripes and plaids with different-size wheels.

Marble-Motion Wrapping Paper

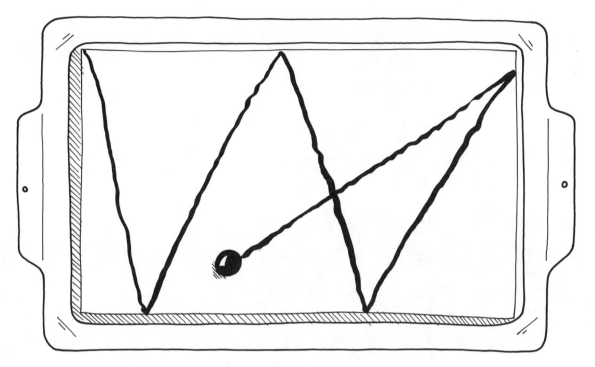

*Children experience and record
motion when they make this project.*

MATERIALS

For each piece of wrapping paper:

Flat-bottomed box or baking sheet with rims

Marbles or small balls (If you are using a large box, you can try larger balls.)

Liquid tempera paints

Butcher or shelf paper

Shallow containers for the paint

Scissors

Newspaper

PROCEDURE

1. Cover the work area with newspaper.

2. Cut the paper to fit inside the bottom of the box or baking sheet.

3. Have the child dip a marble or ball in the paint and drop it on the paper.

4. Let the child move the marble by having him or her move the box back and forth.

5. Have the child dip another marble in another color, and repeat the process.

6. When the paper is finished, remove it from the box and let it dry.

HELPFUL HINTS

For toddlers: With this age group it is best to use a box with high sides that will keep the marble contained.

For primary grades: These children should be able to cut the paper to fit the box.

Foil-and-Tissue Wrapping Paper

This wrapping paper is particularly lovely when placed under a Christmas tree. The lights on the tree reflect off the foil and create a beautiful glow.

MATERIALS

For each piece of wrapping paper:

One 18″ × 25″ piece heavy-duty aluminum foil

Colored tissue paper

White glue

Glue brush

Newspaper

PROCEDURE

1. Cover the work area with newspaper.

2. Have the child cut or tear the tissue paper into small pieces, strips, or geometric shapes.

3. Thin glue slightly with water so that it spreads easily with a brush.

4. Have the child brush small amounts of glue onto the foil and place pieces of tissue on top of the glue. Allow to dry.

HELPFUL HINTS

For toddlers: You may need to help glue the tissue paper down. You might also keep a wet cloth handy for sticky fingers.

For preschoolers: This age group can complete this activity with a small amount of guidance.

For primary grades: You might encourage these children to make patterns on their foil.

Dip-and-Dye Wrapping Paper

This is a wonderful color-mixing activity, and the paper looks like it's been tie-dyed.

MATERIALS

For each piece of wrapping paper:

One sheet of tissue paper

Food coloring or Easter egg dye

Shallow containers for the dye

Water

Newspaper

PROCEDURE

1.   Cover work area with newspaper.

2.   Have the child fold the paper several times. For example, the paper could be folded back and forth to make a fan, and then folded into triangles. The folds should be pressed firmly. (See Figure A.)

3.   Have the child dip each corner into a dye color. Encourage the child to mix colors.

4.   When all the dipping is done, the child should carefully unfold the paper and spread it out on the newspaper to dry.

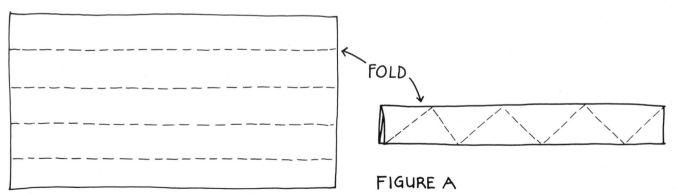

FOLD

FIGURE A

Finger-Paint Wrapping Paper

Children of all ages should experience the delicious mess of finger paints. In this project, the finished artwork is used to wrap a gift.

MATERIALS

For each piece of wrapping paper:

One piece finger-paint paper

Finger paints or dry tempera mixed with liquid starch

Newspaper

PROCEDURE

1. Cover work area with newspaper.

2. Have children drop some finger paint directly on the paper—three or four tablespoon-size drops will do for a start.

3. Have children create designs with their fingers and hands. Make sure they spread the paint thinly over the paper. If there are any large globs of paint in one spot, or if the paper gets too wet, the paint will crack when it is dry.

4. When children are satisfied with their design, allow the paint to dry.

HELPFUL HINTS

For toddlers and preschoolers: You might have children make some handprints with the paints. This makes an appealing wrapping paper for family members.

Sponge-Wash Wrapping Paper

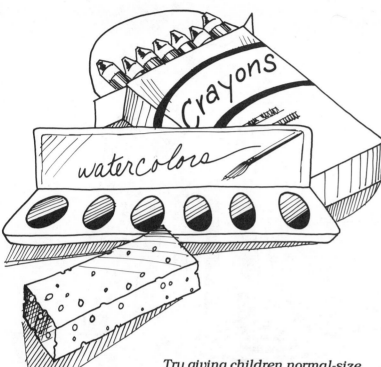

Try giving children normal-size crayons when they do this project.

MATERIALS

For each piece of wrapping paper:

One 9″ × 12″ piece butcher paper

Crayons

Several 3″ × 2½″ pieces of sponge (one for each color)

Watercolors

Containers

Newspaper

PROCEDURE

1. Cover the work area with newspaper.

2. Have the child draw on the paper with the crayons. Encourage him or her to make bold, thick marks.

3. Dilute the watercolors with water in the containers.

4. Have each child dip the sponge in the container and squeeze out the excess liquid.

5. Have the child "brush" the sponge across the paper. The more this is done, the darker the background color will be.

6. Allow the wrapping paper to dry.

VARIATION

• Have the children make "magic" wrapping paper. Have them use only white crayons. When the paint is sponged across the paper, the picture will appear.

Marbled Wrapping Paper

This technique produces marvelous swirling patterns like the grain of polished marble.

MATERIALS

For marbling process:

Eight cups water

One cup rice

Saucepan

Hot plate

For each piece of wrapping paper:

One 8½″ × 11″ piece white paper

Enamel paints or oil-based inks

One 9″ × 13″ disposable baking pan

Small wood sticks, old pencil, or straw

Newspaper

PROCEDURE

1. Put the rice and the water in the saucepan. Boil for 5–7 minutes. Drain the water into the baking pan. (You will no longer need the rice.)

2. Cover the work area with newspaper.

3. Have the child carefully drip some enamel or ink on top of the water. The easiest way to do this is to get a little bit of paint on a stick and then flick it onto the water.

4. Have the child swirl a stick or pencil around in the water to merge the colors.

5. Have the child gently rest the paper on top of the water. Then have the child lift the paper carefully and set it on some newspaper to dry.

Appendix

Recipes and Patterns

Homemade Stamp Pads

MATERIALS

Option 1

Container with lid

Sponge

Six teaspoons food coloring

Two teaspoons rubbing alcohol

One teaspoon water

Option 2

Container with lid

Sponge

Tempera paints

Option 3

Container with lid

Sponge

Bottled ink

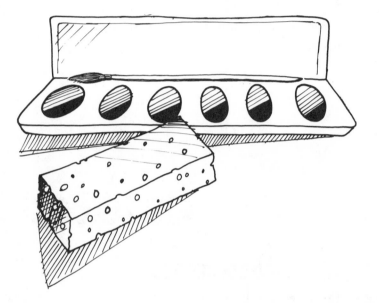

PROCEDURE

1. Cut sponge to fit the bottom of the container.

2. Mix the ingredients together.

3. Pour the mixture over the sponge.

4. Cover the container until ready to use.

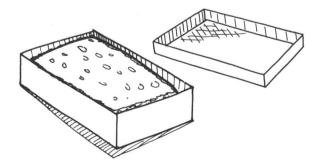

Colored Sand

MATERIALS

Container with lid
One pint sand
4–8 drops food coloring

PROCEDURE

1. Pour sand into the container.
2. Add food coloring.
3. Place lid on container and shake until all of the sand is colored.

Colored Pasta

MATERIALS

Container with lid
One pint pasta (any shape)
Two teaspoons food coloring
Three teaspoons rubbing alcohol
Cookie sheet

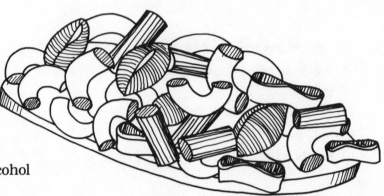

PROCEDURE

1. Mix the food coloring and rubbing alcohol together in the container.
2. Add the pasta and cover with lid.
3. Slowly shake the container, making sure you cover all the pasta with color.
4. Spread the pasta on the cookie sheet in a single layer. Allow to dry for several hours.
5. Store in a tightly covered container.

Dried Flowers

MATERIALS

Heavy books
Collection of various flowers, weeds, and grasses
Five 8½″ × 11″ pieces corrugated cardboard
Newspaper
Strong rubber bands

PROCEDURE

1. Cut about 40 pieces of newspaper to the same size as the cardboard.

2. To press the flowers, lay several pieces of newspaper on top of a piece of cardboard. Lay a flower on top of the newspaper. Cover the flower with more newspaper, and then another piece of cardboard.

3. Repeat the process until all the flowers or the boards are used up.

4. Use the rubber bands to hold the press together.

5. Place the books on top of the press and leave for about a week.

6. Undo the press and remove the flowers.

Calendar Grid Pattern

	Sun.	Mon.	Tues.	Wed.	Thurs.	Fri.	Sat.

From Kids with Love, © 1987 David S. Lake Publishers

Coin Purse Patterns

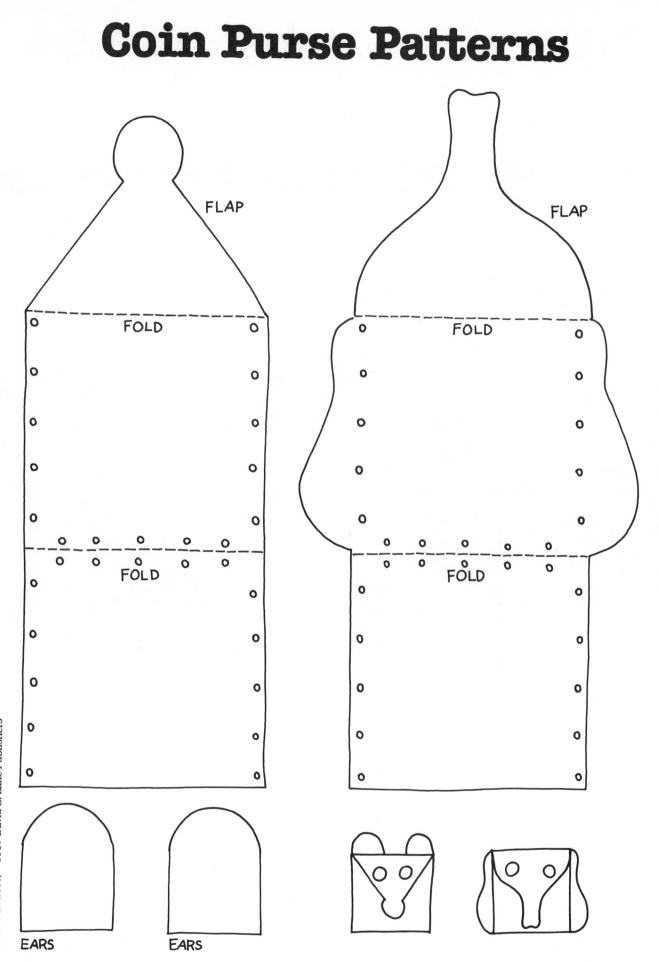

FLAP

FLAP

FOLD

FOLD

FOLD

FOLD

EARS

EARS

Glitter Ornament Patterns

From Kids with Love, © 1987 David S. Lake Publishers